Bradwell's
ECLECT
Greater
MANCHESTER

CW00594811

Published by Bradwell Books
9 Orgreave Close Sheffield S13 9NP
Email: books@bradwellbooks.co.uk

British Library Cataloguing in Publication Data:
a catalogue record for this book is available from
the British Library.

1st Edition

ISBN: 9781909914216

Print: Gutenberg Press, Malta

Design and artwork by: Andrew Caffrey

Photograph Credits: Shutterstock,
Creative Commons, Andy & Sue Caffrey,
and Lancashire archives

Images marked ML. Courtesy of Manchester
Libraries, Information and Archives,
Manchester City Council

Mapping: Ordnance Survey mapping used under
Ordnance Survey Partner Number 100039353

Bibliography

Read on for more information . . .

Introduction

www.buzzfeed.com; http://news.o2.co.ukhttp://
gouk; http://metro.co.uk; www.manchester2002-
uk.com; www.virtualtourist.com; http://
mancunian.askdefine.com; http://englishesna1d.
wikispaces.com; www.bbc.co.uk/manchester;
ww.mysteriousbritain.co.uk; http://murderpedia.
org; www.truecrimelibrary.com; http://www.
chorleyhistorysociety.co.uk; http://news.sky.com;
www.historytoday.com; www.selectsurname.com;
www.hauntedrooms.co.uk; http://hauntedlocations.
net; www.salfordcommunityleisure.co.uk;
http://forums.canadiancontent.net; www.
paranormaldatabase.com; http://allrecipes.
co.uk; www.bbcgoodfood.com; http://britishfood.
about.com; www.prideofmanchester.com; www.
triposo.com; www.demotix.com; http://images.
manchester.gov.uk; www.historicalkits.co.uk; www.
awsomesports.co.uk; http://manchesterexboxers.
co.uk; http://theboar.org; www.localhistories.org;
http://en.wikipedia.org; www.manchester.com;
http://hattersgroup.com; www.visitmanchester.
com; www.localhistories.org; www.world-guides.
com; www.britannica.com; www.phm.org.uk; www.
express.co.uk; http://newbrushcleaning.co.uk; www.
manchester.gov.uk; www.manchester-celebrities.
co.uk; www.manchestereveningnews.co.uk; www.
manchesterconfidential.co.uk; www.manchester-
celebrities.co.uk;http://manchester.y3u.co.uk

Bradwell's ECLECTICA

Greater MANCHESTER

Camilla-Brook-Chorlton

BRADWELL
BOOKS

Contents

WALKS

Take a trip around Manchester's historic heartland and the fascinating Salford Quays with two easy-to-follow walks.

LOCAL CUSTOMS

With such a rich history, it's hardly surprising that Manchester celebrates some intriguing old customs. Get to know just some of them here.

LOCAL HISTORY

Manchester has played an important part in the history of Britain and the world. Read on to learn how its influences have shaped everything from science to workers' rights to industry to music!

SHUTTERSTOCK/LARIO TUS

GHOST STORIES

White ladies, spinning mummy statues, ghostly pub visitors, actorly apparitions . . . there's no doubt about it, Manchester is packed to the rafters with tales of the supernatural! Read on, if you dare!

LOCAL SPORTS

No prizes for naming Manchester's best-known sports team. . . But there's even more to the city than a football team with a global following of over 659 million adults, as you'll soon discover!

SHUTTERSTOCK/FEATUREFLASH

FAMOUS LOCALS

Manchester is the birthplace and the starting point for many famous names, whether you're thinking about the world of science, celebrity, art or sport!

INTRODUCTION

'MANCHESTER IS THE BELLY AND GUTS OF THE NATION'

GEORGE ORWELL

Think Manchester and what do you think of? The industrial powerhouse that led the way in the Industrial Revolution? The birthplace of countless music acts that have gone on to become household names? Or perhaps you think of the football teams and players which have helped make Manchester a popular city around the world . . . Manchester is without doubt a city with many faces, from its industrial roots right through to its continuing place on the world stage. No wonder that Britons voted Manchester 'Britain's Second City' in a national survey in 2013!

In this book I've aimed to show how Manchester manages to have both its industrious and its inventive side. Perhaps it's this mix of the quirky and the committed that lies behind the many scientific breakthroughs which have their origin in Manchester. Perhaps it's why the city has seen so much commercial progress. It could also be why Manchester has played a big part in the development of radical movements which have helped to improve life for people on a much wider scale, from the co-operative movement

to the Suffragettes to the start of the trade unions. Manchester has a fascinating past, as you'll see from this book. But Manchester's future is pretty exciting too. It has the fastest growing economy outside of London with a GDP of £28 billion and it is home to over 2,000 foreign enterprises (source: Metro). Manchester is also the third-most visited city in the UK by foreign visitors, after London and Edinburgh (source: BBC).

Manchester seems to be a place where interesting things keep on happening – not just in terms of great sporting achievements or its continuing contribution to the music scene. There's also the matter of the spinning mummy of Manchester Museum and the recent apparition in a pub in Bolton, both stories reported widely in the international press. Not forgetting the curious fact that Manchester has been acknowledged as something of a UFO sighting hotspot by the Ministry of Defence!

Britain's Second City has brought many firsts to the world. From the very first free public library to the start of the Vegetarianism movement to the first mill to use steam power, it is Manchester that has led the way in so many areas. Manchester is the home of the UK's oldest symphony orchestra, the world's first professional football league and the first steam passenger railway! There's more. The world's very first Co-operative Society was established in Rochdale in 1844! It's extraordinary that one city could give rise to Rolls-Royce, Marks & Spencer and the TUC. Or that one place could have contributed so much to science, such as the discovery of the First Law of Thermodynamics and other ground-breaking discoveries including atomic theory, meteorology and colour blindness, to name but a few. Or that the first computer with a stored programme and memory was developed at Manchester University in 1948. It's a history which is recorded brick by brick in Manchester's incredible architecture, from the Victoria Baths

to Albert Square. We've included two walks to give a quick snapshot of all that Manchester's buildings and other sights have to offer. Perhaps you'll get a chance to practise a little Mancunian by using the dialect guide in this book, whether you're asking for a 'chip butty' or you want to let people know how 'made up' you are to be visiting the city. From 'Cottonopolis' to 'the Chimney of the World' to 'Madchester' to 'Britain's Second City', Manchester has had many identities. There's so much to say about Manchester and so little time to do it in this short book. My advice? Take a peek around this book and, if it inspires you, why not take a trip to Manchester? If you know it already, you'll find there's always more to discover. I would go further than George Orwell's quotation shown earlier. Manchester isn't just about belly and guts. It's about heart, too.

MANCHESTER is renowned for its distinctive accent and quirky phrases. Who can forget the phrase **'mad for it'**, as made famous in the era of the Stone Roses and the Happy Mondays? Or what about **'Let's crack on'**, which seems to be in popular use in many parts of the country nowadays? While some of the words and phrases are somewhat old and out of everyday use, others are more popular than ever!

Have you ever wondered what it means to be **'cabbaged'**, what **'heads'** are and why you would want to have a **'raz'** time when you're visiting Manchester? Or would you like to discover why

Mancunians sometimes feel like **their stomach thinks their throat's been cut** or why it's not great news when something's **'bobbins'** or why you wouldn't want to be called a **'gonk'**?

With this distinctive dialect, it's entertaining to learn that **'gravy'** isn't just something you put on your food, that **'gigs'** aren't just events with live music and that you wouldn't want to forget your **'Salfords'** when you're visiting Manchester in the depths of winter!

Read on to test your knowledge of Mancunian! Nice one!

A

Ace – very good
Alright? – how are you?
'Angin' – (hanging) disgusting, not nice
'Ave a word – to have a talk with someone; to put them 'right'

B

Bang on – perfect
Bap – bread roll
Barm – bread roll
Barmy – mad/eccentric
Barney – argument
Bessies – best friends
Blimey! – exclamation of amazement
Blinder – something great
Blinding – very good
Bloke – man
Blud – friend/brother
Bobbins – rubbish/not good
Bob off – to leave
Bob on! – that's correct! Dead right
Bobby – police officer
Bog – toilet
Booze – alcoholic drink

C

Cabbaged – confused, messed up
Champion – good
Cheers – thank you
Chillin' – relaxing
Chill out – relax
Chilly – cold
Chinwag – chat
Chip muffin – chip butty
Chip off – to leave
Chippy – fish and chip shop
Chuck it – throw it away
Chuddy/chud – chewing gum
Cob – bread roll
Cock – mate or friend

D

Daft 'apeth – fool, idiot
Dead – very, extremely
Dibble – the police
Digits – number
Dope – really good

Down our end – where we live
Dry – boring

E

Epic – good

F

Fettle – fix or repair

G

Gaggin' – very thirsty or desperate
Gaff – home
Gigs – glasses
Ginnel – alleyway through a row of houses
Going off – out of control
Gonk – idiot
Gormless – stupid
Grand – very good
Gravy – good
Gump – foolish person
Gutted – upset, disappointed

H

Heads – people

Hiya – hello
Hotpot – stew

I

Innit? – isn't it?

K

Keks – trousers
Kippered – tired
Knackered – tired

L

Lad – boy/man
Lass – girl
Later(s) – goodbye
Lothered – sweating

M

Madchester – the alternative name for Manchester which developed around its vibrant music scene in the late 1980s/early 1990s
Made up – really happy
Madhead – crazy person
Mad hot – very hot

Mad keen – very enthusiastic
Mardy – bad tempered
Mate – friend
Minging – unclean/unattractive
Mingey – mean
Mint – great, very good
Mither – bother, trouble

N

Newtons – teeth (rhyming slang: Newton Heath – teeth)
Nice one/top one – very good
Nippers – young kids
Nowt – nothing
Nowty – grumpy
Numpty – idiot, stupid person

O

Owt – anything

P

Pal – friend
Peeps – people
Peppered – broke
Poorly – unwell

Pop – fizzy drink
Potato hash – mashed potato and meat
Potty – mad/eccentric
Proper – very
Pure – really good

R

Ragged – messy
Raz! – something's good/great
Right – very
Round of toast – a slice of toast
Rozzer – police officer

S

Safe – OK
Salfords – socks (rhyming slang: Salford Docks – socks)
Sarnie – sandwich
Schnoz – nose
Scran – food
Scrikin' – crying
Sick – good/fantastic
Sis – sister
Skrieking – crying

Slopstone – sink
Smokin' – good
Snide – mean, ungenerous
Soft – silly, stupid
Sound – good or decent
Sorted! – great, all set up
Strop – tantrum
Spanner – a daft person
Spitting – raining lightly
Spuds – potatoes
Summat – something

T

Tenner – ten pounds
Top – good
Trolleys – trousers, underwear
Turn it in – stop it
Tutty – lipstick, make-up

Y

Yard – house
Yoghurt – a person with a confused view of life, or differing views to your own

MANCUNIAN SAYINGS

'My stomach thinks my throat's been cut!' – I'm feeling very hungry!

'Fish, chips and peas with pea wet' – Fish, chips and peas with the water they were cooked in

'What did they cut your hair with, a knife and fork?' – You have a dodgy haircut!

'Nah man' – I don't believe that!

'Swear down . . .' – I'm telling the truth!

'Our kid' – Close friend or sibling

'You don't get owt for nowt' – You can't get something for nothing

'Give your 'ead a wobble' – You need to have a rethink

'You're peckin' me 'ead' – You're annoying me

'Stop ya chattin' – Stop talking a load of rubbish!

'Ave it!' – An exclamation of celebration, usually after a success

'Mind out!' – Be careful!

'Let's crack on' – Let's get on with it

'Get lost!' – Go away!

'Give over!' – Stop it

'In a bit!' – Soon, bye

'Put wood int' 'ole.' – Shut the door

'Me gaff' – My house

'Mad for it' – Over excited, very happy

'Sat here like piffy on a rock' – Sitting waiting around for someone to arrive

'He couldn't stop a pig in a ginnel' – He has bandy legs

'Your hair is full o' lugs' – Your hair is very knotted

'That is bobbins' – That's not very good

'That is well bad' – That's a bad situation; or the opposite, really good!

'Go on a mooch' – Go on a long walk for no particular reason

'Go on a trek/mission' – Go on a really long walk for a reason

'I'm sweating cobs' – I'm really hot

'I haven't the foggiest' – I have no idea

'It was a piece of cake' – It was very easy

'Get yer mad up' – Become angry

'Y' all right? – How are you?

'Yer fibbin'!' – You're lying

'You barmy dog!' – You're very silly

'Mee-maw' – To communicate with a person using a combination of exaggerated facial expressions, sign language and lip reading. This expression apparently refers to the way that mill workers communicated with each other over the noise of the machinery during the Industrial Revolution.

HUMOUR

A COLLECTION OF RIB-TICKLING JOKES FROM MANCHESTER

A strong young man working on a busy Manchester construction site was bragging that he could outdo anyone in a feat of strength. He made a special case of making fun of Morris, one of the older workmen. After several minutes, Morris had had enough.

'Why don't you put your money where your mouth is?' he said. 'I'll bet a week's wages that I can haul something in a wheelbarrow over to that outbuilding that you won't be able to wheel back.'

'You're on, old man,' the boaster replied. 'It's a bet! Let's see what you got.'

Morris reached out and grabbed the wheelbarrow by the handles. Then, nodding to the young man, he said, 'All right. Get in.'

The Beatles wrote a song about Wigan . . .

It's called 'Wigan work it out'!

....

What do you call a Mancunian in a filing cabinet?

Sorted!

....

Why do Northerners prefer mushy peas?

Because they can't keep the round ones on their knives.

....

You know you're a Mancunian when:

You know the four seasons – winter, still winter, not winter and almost winter.

....

You know you're a Mancunian when:

Your dog wears boots too.

A general was inspecting troops in Hampshire and ordered the parade to put on gas masks. He paused opposite a soldier from Manchester. Pointing to the eyepiece of his respirator, he enquired: *'Soldier, where is your anti-mist?' 'Don't know, Sir,'* came the reply. *'Think she's oop with Uncle Albert in Oldham.'*

Ian was having a pint at his local when a loud-mouthed guy called Henry walked in. Ian couldn't help overhearing Henry trying to bet a couple of young lads 50 quid that they couldn't drink 20 pints in 20 minutes. After a lot of cajoling, Henry was unsuccessful in his goal to make a few quid. He looked around at Ian and said, 'Well what about you then? Are you game?' Ian shrugged, downed his pint and left the pub.

Half an hour later Ian walked back into his local and said to Henry, 'I'll take that bet.' Henry smiled at the easy money he would make as Ian began to drink the pints. Henry's smile soon disappeared when Ian polished off the 20 pints in 19 minutes. Handing over the cash, Henry asked, 'When you left the here earlier, where did you go?' Ian looked at him and replied, 'I had to go to the pub down the road to see if I could do it first.'

John was down on his luck so he thought he would try getting a few odd jobs by calling at the posh houses in Wilmslow. After a few said 'no chance', a guy in one of the big houses thought he would give him a break, so he says, 'The porch needs painting. I'll give you £50 to paint it for me.'

'You're a life-saver, mister; I'll get started right away!' Times passes until. . .

'There you go, I'm all done with the painting.'

'Well, here's your £50.'

'Thanks very much. Oh, by the way, it's a Ferrari, not a Porsche!'

Did you hear about the truck driver from Prestwich who was seen desperately chiselling away at the brickwork after his lorry got stuck while passing through a tunnel?

'Why don't you let some air out of your tyres?' asked a helpful passer-by.

'No, mate,' replied the driver. 'It's the roof that won't go under, not the wheels.'

RECIPES

Manchester Tart

Believed to have been created in Manchester in the 1800s, Manchester Tart is well loved as an old staple of school dinners. Even today, Manchester tart is a well-known and popular pudding. Here's how to make it for yourself.

See **page 24** for recipe

Lancashire Hotpot

Closely associated with both Manchester and Lancashire, the Lancashire Hotpot has a proud history. Traditionally a hotpot would be made from either lamb or mutton with onion and covered with sliced potatoes. It would have been created in a very tall and large brown pot. In October 2007 the world's biggest hotpot to date (weighing in at 200kg) was made in Garstang as part of the launch of Taste Lancashire 2008! The Lancashire Hotpot is so important to Lancashire's heritage that it has been in the running to receive protected status. But don't let that stop you from creating your own version of this Northern classic!

INGREDIENTS: SERVES FOUR HUNGRY PEOPLE

55g /2 oz butter, melted
100g beef dripping or lard
900g stewing lamb, cut into large chunks
3 lamb kidneys, sliced, fat removed (optional)
2 medium onions, chopped
2 carrots, peeled and thickly sliced
1 tsp Worcestershire sauce
500ml beef or chicken stock
2 bay leaves
900g potatoes, peeled and thickly sliced

PREPARATION:

1. Heat oven to 200°C/Gas mark 6.
2. In a large frying pan, heat some dripping or butter in a large shallow casserole dish until it's hot, brown the lamb in batches, lift to a plate, drain on kitchen paper, then repeat with the kidneys, if you're including them.
3. Next, add the onions and carrots in the pan with a little more dripping until golden. Remove from the fat and drain on the kitchen paper.
4. Sprinkle over the flour, allow to cook for a couple of minutes, shake over the Worcestershire sauce, pour in the stock, then bring to the boil.
5. Stir in the meat and bay leaves, and then turn off the heat. Arrange the sliced potatoes on top of the meat, and then drizzle with a little more dripping. Cover, then place in the oven for about 1½ hrs until the potatoes are cooked.
6. Remove the lid, brush the potatoes with a little more dripping, then turn the oven up to brown the potatoes, or finish under the grill for 5–8 minutes until brown.
7. After 30 minutes, reduce the heat to 180°C/Gas 4 and cook for a further 1½ hours. Check from time to time to make sure the casserole isn't drying out, and top up with stock or water as necessary.
8. Remove the lid from the casserole and cook until the potatoes on the surface are brown, remove from the oven and leave to rest for about 10 minutes. Serve on hot plates with fresh, seasonal vegetables.

Eccles Cakes

Enjoyed in Manchester, Lancashire and many other parts of the world even today, the Eccles cake is a quirky and delicious classic. Ignore its slightly off-putting nickname of 'squashed fly cake' and have a go at making this tasty treat at home!

INGREDIENTS: SERVES EIGHT PEOPLE

30g unsalted butter
150g currants
2 tablespoons chopped candied mixed fruit peel
50g soft brown sugar
¾ teaspoon mixed spice
1 block of frozen ready-made puff pastry, thawed
1 egg white, beaten
4 tablespoons caster sugar for dusting

PREPARATION:

1. Preheat oven to 220°C / Gas mark 7. Sprinkle a baking tray with water.

2. For the filling, melt the butter over a low heat in a small saucepan. Once melted, remove from the heat and stir in all of the remaining filling ingredients until well combined. Remove from the heat.

3. For the pastry, roll out the pastry on a lightly floured work surface to a thickness of about 5mm. Using a 6cm/2½in cutter, cut the pastry into rounds.

4. Divide the fruit mix equally between three circles, and then brush the edges of half the pastry with milk. Bring the other half of the pastry over and seal. Bring the corners of the pastry up into the middle and pinch to seal.

5. Invert filled cakes on the floured surface and roll out gently to make a wider, flatter circle, but do not break the pastry. Gently pat back into a round shape and place onto the greased baking tray.

6. Cut each cake across three times using the tip of a sharp knife. Brush the cakes with milk and sprinkle generously with caster sugar.

7. Bake in a pre-heated oven for 15 minutes, until the pastry is golden brown and puffed up. Transfer the cakes to a wire rack to cool.

8. Dust the Eccles cakes with icing sugar before serving. Delicious!

MANCHESTER TART

INGREDIENTS: SERVES SIX HUNGRY PEOPLE
1 sheet ready-rolled shortcrust pastry
Butter, for greasing
3 tablespoons of raspberry jam
Plain flour, for dusting
3 tbsp desiccated coconut
Another 3 tbsp desiccated coconut
lightly toasted in a dry frying pan
Make 1 pint/500ml custard using your
favourite brand of powder
Half a teaspoon of vanilla extract to
boost up the custard

PREPARATION:

1. Preheat the oven to 200°C/Gas mark 6.
2. Grease a 24cm round tart tin with butter.
3. Roll out the shortcrust pastry onto a lightly floured work surface to a 0.5cm/¼in thickness. Line the prepared tart tin with the pastry. Prick the pastry several times with a fork, then chill in the fridge for 30 minutes.
4. When the pastry case has rested, place a sheet of baking parchment into it and half-fill with baking beans. Transfer the pastry case to the oven and bake for 15 minutes, or until pale golden-brown around the top.
5. Remove the baking parchment and baking beans and return the pastry case to the oven for a further 4–5 minutes or so until the base is nice and crisp. Set aside to cool.
6. For the custard, use full fat milk and your favourite custard powder, follow the instructions and make it fairly thick so add a tad more powder than the instructions; half a teaspoon of vanilla extract will boost the custard! Allow the custard to cool.
7. Spread jam over the pastry case and sprinkle with half the coconut. Pour in custard, sprinkle with lightly toasted coconut. Chill until ready to serve.

MURDERS

THE BILL O' JACK'S MURDERS

There was widespread horror in response to the Bill o' Jack's murders which took place near Saddleworth in Oldham. A local newspaper called the terrible double murder which took place in 1832 'one of the most diabolical murders ever committed'. Another reason the murders were so shocking is that they took place in a pub, a place where you would least expect such brutality to take place. Sadly, hundreds of years on, the Bill o' Jack's murders still remain unsolved.

The tragic events took place at the remote Moorcock Inn on a quiet moorland above Greenfield, near Saddleworth. William Bradbury was the landlord of the Moorcock Inn and Thomas, his son, was a gamekeeper. Both were discovered to have been attacked, with signs of a violent struggle throughout the pub. William survived long enough to whisper the word 'pats' as a clue to his attackers, but despite several theories about this clue and a £100 reward, the murderers were never found.

Today, while the Moorcock Inn is long gone, you can still visit the local church and see the gravestone which commemorates the terrible murders with the words:

Here lie the dreadfully bruised and lacerated bodies of William Bradbury and Thomas, his son, both of Greenfield, who were together savagely murdered in an unusually horrid manner, on Monday night, April 2nd 1832, William being 84 and Thomas 46 years old.

Throughout the land wherever news is read Intelligence of their sad end has spread. Those now who talk of far-famed Greenfield hills.
Will think of Bill o' Jack's and Tom o' Bill's. Such interest did their tragic end excite.

The gravestone tells the sad story MANCHESTER LIBRARIES

That, ere they were removed from

human sight.

Thousands on thousands came to see.

The bloody scene of catastrophe.

One house, one business, and one bed.

And one most shocking death they had.

One funeral came, one inquest past.

And now one grave they had a last.

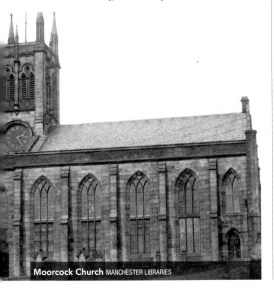

Moorcock Church MANCHESTER LIBRARIES

MARY ANN BRITLAND AND THE 'MOUSE POWDER' MURDERS

In 1886, **Mary Ann Britland** earned the unwanted honour of being the first woman to be executed by hanging at Manchester's Strangeways Prison. Born in Bolton, Mary Ann seemed to have a normal life by most people's standards. So why was it that one day, after purchasing some specialist poisons to rid her Ashton-under-Lyne home of a mouse infestation, Mary Ann used them to murder her daughter, nineteen-year-old Elizabeth Hannah? Sadly, signs of the crime were not spotted by the doctor who examined poor Elizabeth, and Mary Ann was eventually able to claim £10 on her life insurance policy.

Mary Ann's next victim was her husband, Thomas. Once again, his death was not deemed to be suspicious and Mary Ann was able to claim on his life insurance. But it didn't end there . . . Mary Ann had been having an

Strangeways Prison MANCHESTER LIBRARIES

affair with her neighbour, also called Thomas (Dixon). Thomas's wife kindly invited Mary Ann to stay at their home after the death and what was her reward? To be murdered by Mary Ann. This time, the authorities realised that the pattern of events was more than a little bit suspicious and Mary Ann was arrested. She eventually confessed to the police that she had had hopes of becoming Thomas Dixon's wife. She had murdered her daughter Elizabeth because Elizabeth had suspected this plan. The trial lasted just two days and Mary Ann became the first woman to be hanged at Strangeways.

THE PLUMBER-MURDERER

John Jackson gained great notoriety in the 1800s due to a strange chain of events which led to a tragic murder. So what was it that drove a plumber and petty criminal to go on to be executed for murder? Jackson, who was a plumber by trade, was in Wakefield Prison for the theft of a horse during his time in the army. He did manage to escape from prison, but was eventually sent back.

He served his time for the theft and was released. But this was not for long. After being arrested for breaking into homes in Manchester, Jackson was sent to Strangeways Prison. But his talents as a plumber had not gone unrecognised.

While still in prison, Jackson was asked to deal with a gas leak in the home of the prison matron and was escorted there by a warder called Webb. Once he had done his work, Jackson suddenly attacked and killed Webb with a hammer. He then stole Webb's boots and escaped through the attic.

Jackson lived as a fugitive for a few weeks, breaking into homes for food and other supplies. When he was eventually caught, he confessed to the murder and was hanged at Strangeways.

THE WIGAN MURDERER

The Wigan Murderer became infamous after terrible events which took place in 1863, attracting the attention of Queen Victoria herself! The location for this murder was Button Pit, a small colliery in Haigh. One day at dawn, a miner went searching for a colleague who had mysteriously gone missing. He suddenly noticed a substance which looked like blood on the door of the colliery's furnace . . . He looked inside to discover white ash. This turned out to be the remains of James Barton. Poor Barton had been the caretaker of the colliery as well as a part-time gamekeeper. He had been beaten before being thrown into the furnace. While there was a great deal of speculation about the reason for the murder, nothing conclusive was uncovered.

One possible motive for the murder was Barton's watch, which had been considered to be valuable. The search for the murderer went on for three years without any real leads. The case was followed by the entire country. A £300 reward was offered for any information that could be provided, a significant amount in Victorian times. Queen Victoria also issued a pardon for any accomplice who was able to provide information. The police then tried to encourage a response by

Queen Victoria SHUTTERSTOCK/OLEG GOLOVNEV

giving a detailed summary of Barton's watch in the local papers. This time, something did happen.

A man called James Grime read the description and suddenly remembered his brother, Thomas, showing him his new watch, which looked very similar . . . He rushed off to the pawn shop where his brother had taken the watch, bought it back and then went to the police. The irony was that Thomas Grime was already in prison at the time . . . for stealing a horse blanket. He was no stranger to the police, due to his career in petty crime. At first Grime confessed to the murder, but then changed his story, saying that while he had been present at the murder, he had not committed the crime himself. He did give the names of the people he alleged were responsible for the murder, but the police couldn't find any proof.

The man who became known as

SHUTTERSTOCK/VOLODYMYR BURDIAK

The Wigan Murderer went on to be hanged in Liverpool before a crowd of 50,000 onlookers. However, many people were not satisfied with the trial. Despite these doubts, the name and the story of The Wigan Murderer live on to this day.

WALTER GRAHAM ROWLAND

A World War II bomb site was the location of the discovery of another notorious murder in Manchester. In 1947, the body of a woman called Olive Balchin was found. Her skull had been crushed with a hammer. The hammer, of a kind which was used in the leather-making process, was discovered nearby. Local people were able to provide the police with descriptions of a man who had been seen with Olive before her death.

The police were particularly keen to talk to a man called Rowland who had previously been convicted of murder. Some believed that Rowland and Balchin had been romantically involved, while another theory was that Olive was a prostitute. The odd thing was that Rowland had had a strong alibi for the night of Balchin's murder, yet forensic examinations placed him at the scene of the crime. His alibi was that he was at a local pub.

This was backed up by an off-duty policeman who had also been drinking in the pub at the time. However, on the basis of the forensic evidence, Rowland was arrested. The sad story of Olive Balchin's murder doesn't end there. While Rowland was facing the prospect of execution, a man called David Ware, who was in Strangeways for robbery, confessed to Olive's murder. On further examination, he was shown to be lying and took back his confession.

Rowland was then hanged for the murder. David Ware went on to attack another woman in 1951. This time he was found to be guilty, but also insane.

LOCAL NAMES

The Bayeux Tapestry SHUTTERSTOCK/JORISVO

NORMAN ROOTS

The Norman Conquest shaped the history of many Manchester and Greater Manchester families. In fact, there are Manchester families today that can follow their ancestry right back to 1066!

Norman Ship SHUTTERSTOCK/MORPHART CREATION

THE AINSWORTHS OF HALLIWELL

Textile bleaching may not be big business these days, but it was important enough to create a hugely successful family enterprise which helped influence the history of Greater Manchester. The Ainsworth family made Halliwell their home in the 1700s. Peter Ainsworth was a pioneer in chemical bleaching, setting up the Halliwell bleach works in 1739. The

SHUTTERSTOCK/KARIN HILDEBRAND LAU

family made such a success of their business that they became extremely prosperous and influential in the area. It was said that Peter Ainsworth was known locally as 'the opulent bleacher'. But these businesspeople wanted to be benefactors too. The Ainsworth fortune and name lies behind new schools, farms and other developments in the area and is an important aspect of Manchester's history.

THE MOSLEYS OF MANCHESTER

The world of business lies behind another old and successful Manchester name. This time it was the manufacturing of woollen cloth which helped make the name Mosley synonymous with Manchester. The Mosley history also includes the provision of shelter to the Young Pretender at the family home of Ancoats Hall in Manchester. The family continued to make their name when Nicholas Mosley became Lord of the Manor of Manchester and also Lord Mayor of London! This Manchester man also supported Queen Elizabeth I in her fight against the Spanish Armada and went on to

Queen Elizabeth I SHUTTERSTOCK/GEORGIOS KOLLIDAS

be knighted. Sir Nicholas also built Hough End Hall in Manchester.

THE BRIGHTS OF ROCHDALE AND JOHN BRIGHT

The Brights were a large family from Rochdale. While they had a relatively modest background, being Quaker cotton spinners, the father of the family managed to work his way up to become the owner of his own cotton mill. His son, John Bright, who was born in 1811, went on to become a leading Victorian radical and Liberal politician.

John Bright SHUTTERSTOCK/ANTONIO ABRIGNANI

SHAPED BY IMMIGRANTS

Glasgow School of Art SHUTTERSTOCK/ARTONO

It's not just old families that have helped to shape Manchester into the place it is today. Manchester has been greatly influenced by many generations of immigrants. This first started when people came from all over England and Ireland to work in the city's many factories as part of its industrial growth. In the late nineteenth century, Manchester was enriched again with Italians and Jewish East Europeans. After the Second World War, Manchester became home to refugees from Europe. Later on, the city welcomed people from the ex-colonies of the British Empire. It was from the 1950s onwards that Manchester became home to African-Caribbean and Pakistani people. The Hallé Orchestra, which had its beginnings in Manchester, was first funded by businessmen of German origin. Today, more than 200 languages are spoken in Manchester in a city which has been hailed as 'the winner of immigration'.

WALKS

EXPLORING MANCHESTER AND SALFORD QUAYS

CITY CENTRE WALK
Duration: 50 minutes (approx)
Distance: 2.2 miles (3.5 km)

This walk around the centre of Manchester takes in some of its impressive architecture and industrial heritage, and gives a flavour both of the city's rich and varied past and of the lively, cosmopolitan metropolis that it has become today.

1. The walk starts from Albert Square with its imposing Town Hall, designed by Alfred Waterhouse in the Victorian neo-gothic style and completed in 1877.

2. Cross the road into the pedestrianised Brazennose Street, heading towards Deansgate, passing the hidden gem of St Mary's Catholic Church on your

The Town Hall ANDY/SUSAN CAFFREY

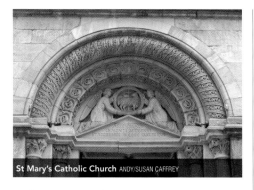

St Mary's Catholic Church ANDY/SUSAN CAFFREY

right and walking through Lincoln Square with Abraham Lincoln's statue on your left.

3. Turn left onto Deansgate, noting the interesting bronze of Chopin at his piano. Carefully cross Deansgate,

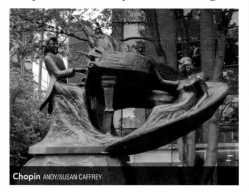

Chopin ANDY/SUSAN CAFFREY

looking for the next right turn (Hardman Street).

4. Walk down Hardman Street. You are now entering Spinningfields, a modern, interesting area full of restaurants and bars. Follow the pedestrian way to the left with the Long Bar on your left and Carluccios on your right, through to Gartside Street. Cross Quay Street onto Lower Byrom Street (noting the sign pointing the way to the Science Museum – your next destination).

Spinningfields ANDY/SUSAN CAFFREY

5. You will find the Museum of Science and Industry (MOSI) on your right and the imposing Air and Space Hall on your left.

Air and Space Hall ANDY/SUSAN CAFFREY

6. Turn left into Liverpool Road, then right into the Roman gardens at Castlefield with the White Lion pub on your left. You are now in Roman Manchester with the remains of a Roman fort and ditch.

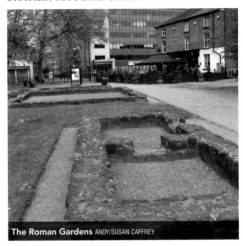

The Roman Gardens ANDY/SUSAN CAFFREY

7. Continue through the Fort arches and turn right onto the cobbled road Beaufort Street, then go left towards the railway arches – noting on your right the Roman granary and the plaque on the wall depicting 'A Slice of History'.

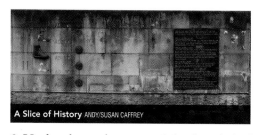

A Slice of History ANDY/SUSAN CAFFREY

8. Under the arches turn right then left at Barça along the cobbled way: this is Catalan Square, an attractive place to stop by the canal for food and drink.

9. Turn left (Castle Street) and arrive at a red-and-cream-coloured railway bridge; the impressive 47-storey Beetham Tower is facing you. Go under the bridge and cross over to Whitworth Street West with Deansgate Station on your right. Continue until the next traffic lights and cross to the Haçienda apartments, once the site of the famous Haçienda music venue, labelled the most famous club in the world by Newsweek magazine.

10. Turn left here along Albion Street and continue to Great Bridgewater Street with the Britons Protection pub on the corner. Turn right here, passing the back entrance for the famous

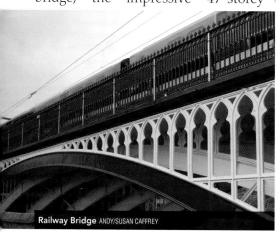

Railway Bridge ANDY/SUSAN CAFFREY

Deansgate Station ANDY/SUSAN CAFFREY

Bridgewater Concert Hall, continue to the Peveril of the Peak pub and pass to the left of it onto Chepstow Street. Follow to the next traffic lights and turn left onto Oxford Street. Head towards the magnificent Central Library with the famous red-brick Midland Hotel on your left. You are now on Peter Street; take the next right onto Mount Street to return to Albert Square and the start of your walk.

Peveril of the Peak pub ANDY/SUSAN CAFFREY

The Midland Hotel ANDY/SUSAN CAFFREY

The Lowry Centre ANDY/SUSAN CAFFREY

SALFORD QUAYS WALK

Duration: 50 minutes (approx)
Distance: 2.2 miles (3.5 km)

This short walk takes you around some of the main buildings and dock sides in Salford Quays. You may start from a number of locations including the Imperial War Museum North (IWM) or the Media City Tram Terminus. We start at the famous Lowry Centre. There is plenty of parking at the Lowry Centre Mall car park.

1. With your back to the Lowry Centre, looking across the plaza, to your right you will see the Lowry Bridge that crosses the Manchester Ship Canal. As you cross the bridge you will have impressive views to your right and left of the spectacular development that has taken place in Salford Quays in recent times, including the BBC and ITV studios at MediaCity. Straight ahead is the eye-catching bronze Quay West Building.

The Lowry Bridge ANDY/SUE CAFFREY

2. Once over the bridge, turn right and follow one of the several paths that run by the old Manchester Ship Canal, once packed with shipping but scarcely used today. If you are starting from the IWM car park then bear left. You should head to the dramatic footbridge that crosses back over the canal and leads you into the MediaCity complex.

Footbridge leading to MediaCity ANDY/SUSAN CAFFREY

3. Continue straight ahead through MediaCity, and see if you can spot any celebrities! When you come to a large courtyard bear right and pick up the path by the side of the North Bay.

MediaCity ANDY/SUSAN CAFFREY

Here is the Media City Tram Terminus, which is where you may want to start this walk if you are touring the city by tram. At the end of the path cross the road and continue straight on with the Huron Basin on your right. The water here is considered so clean that people swim in it during the summer months

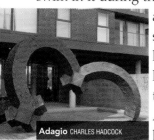

Adagio CHARLES HADCOCK

and there are also swimming events held here. On your left you will see the spectacular **Adagio** sculpture by Charles Hadcock.

4. Head towards the Detroit Bridge that divides this dock into the Erin Basin and the Huron Basin and is the turning point of this walk. Once over the bridge turn right and follow the path back to the road and then take a left back to where you started at the Lowry Centre. Or if you started at the IWM or the tram terminus, go back to point 1 and carry on to your start point. Time now for tea, coffee or some retail therapy.

The Detroit Bridge ANDY/SUSAN CAFFREY

GHOST STORIES

THE HEADLESS DOG

Back in the early 1800s, local people used to terrify each other with tales of the headless dog which haunted Manchester's streets! Many locals claimed to have spotted the canine phantom around Manchester Cathedral.

WYTHENSHAWE HALL

It is said that Manchester's great houses play host to many kinds of otherworldly visitors. One such location for rumoured hauntings is Wythenshawe Hall, a 16th-century historic house and former stately home in Wythenshawe. A particularly active apparition is known as Mary

SHUTTERSTOCK/LARIO TUS

Webb or the Lady in White. Mary has been spotted on a number of occasions over the years. In the 1990s, visitors were happily looking around the hall when they heard the sound of a woman crying. They then noticed a woman in white walking along the corridor and into a bedroom. They were excited, thinking it was perhaps some kind of historical re-enactment. But when they followed the figure into the room, they were shocked to find it empty! The ghost is thought to be that of Mary Webb, who worked as a servant at Wythenshawe Hall in the 1600s. Her cries are believed to hark back to her fearful reaction just before Parliamentarians attacked the hall and killed her and her fiancé.

It's not just the Lady in White who is thought to keep vigil at Wythenshawe Hall. Employees have experienced odd phenomena, such as the sound of mysterious footsteps and even gunfire! Who can explain the story of the employees who were walking downstairs when a large tapestry came off the wall over the staircase and landed on them? Then there's the library. It's not just home to old books. People have heard odd dragging sounds coming from there.

Monks too have made an appearance

Wythenshawe Hall MANCHESTER LIBRARIES

Ye Olde Man and Scythe SHUTTERSTOCK/TUPUNGATO

at the hall. According to another real-life ghost story, two friends were cutting across the grounds of the hall on their way home when they saw a group of monks standing in front of them . . . But what was even odder was the monks were missing the bottom half of their legs, as if they were walking on a lower level. As the two men watched in horror, the monks faded away in front of them!

THE HAUNTING OF THE YE OLDE MAN AND SCYTHE

Manchester has a long history of hauntings, yet one particularly high-profile appearance is still making the news today! In 2014, the national press was full of stories about the creepy entity which was thought to haunt the Ye Olde Man and Scythe Pub in Bolton. As the fourth oldest pub in Britain, dating all the way back to 1251, you would expect it to have more than a little bit of history. Yet there was a massive public reaction when a purported ghost was thought to have been captured on CCTV on Friday 14 February 2014. The camera footage seems to show a shadowy figure standing by the bar.

More used to dealing with the other kind of spirits, the pub's manager noticed the weird figure when he checked the pub's cameras on Friday

James Stanley SHUTTERSTOCK/GEORGIOS KOLLIDAS

morning and found a broken glass on the pub floor. Oddly enough, the cameras had stopped recording at 6.18am in the morning . . . So who is this ghostly figure? Well, Ye Olde Man and Scythe is said to boast no fewer than 25 regulars from beyond the grave. But there is one specific contender: James Stanley, 7th Earl of Derby. Some 400 years ago, in 1651, James Stanley was beheaded right outside the pub for his role in the Bolton Massacre, the only massacre of the English Civil War. In fact, Stanley had his final meal in the pub. Was this a special message from Stanley or some other figure from the past? We'll probably never know.

THE SPINNING MUMMY OF MANCHESTER MUSEUM

Manchester has been connected with yet another modern-day apparition, this time in 2013 when the statue of a mummy was seen to spin! The international press was full of tales of the 10-inch-tall statue of a man called Neb-Senu. The statue was originally created as an offering to the god Osiris, but has stood (still) in the museum for 80 years. So why was it suddenly seen to face a different way in its cabinet? A curator at the museum decided to set up a time-lapse camera to check what was happening and the video clearly shows the statue moving on its own! One theory is that vibrations from the flooring are causing the statue to move. But the statue has stood in the same place for 80 years, so what would make it move now – otherworldly forces or plain old physics? Either way, the spinning mummy has raised Manchester's profile even higher.

SHUTTERSTOCK/JOSE IGNACIO SOTO

Ordsall Hall MANCHESTER LIBRARIES

ORDSALL HALL

Explore many a stately home in Greater Manchester and you'll soon hear of a ghost or two. A great example of this is Ordsall Hall in Salford. If you believe the stories (and the photographs) this Grade I listed Tudor Mansion is packed to the rafters with unquiet spirits of all kinds! Locals and visitors have heard and seen all kinds of apparently inexplicable things. No wonder an episode of the popular TV show Most Haunted was filmed in the Hall in 2004. You can watch for ghostly happenings yourself thanks to the Hall's three ghost cams, giving online access to its supernatural side in the oldest and most haunted parts of the Hall from 5pm to 8am every night. The ghost cams are now watched by more than 30,000 people a month!

THE WHITE LADY

If you're at Ordsall Hall and you notice a woman in white walking the halls with a candle in her hand, you may well be encountering one of its most high-profile ghosts, the White Lady. There are many theories about the identity of this mysterious figure. According to some, the White Lady of Ordsall Hall is **Queen Elizabeth I** herself. Another theory is that she is Margaret Radclyffe, Queen Elizabeth

I's favourite Maid of Honour, who died in 1599 from a broken heart following the death of her brother. Yet another theory suggests that the White Lady is the apparition of a bride who was jilted at the altar and leapt to her death from the Great Hall. Or could she be Viviana Radclyffe, with whom the infamous Guy Fawkes fell in love when he supposedly came to Ordsall Hall to devise the Gunpowder Plot? Whoever she is, the White Lady of Ordsall now has her own Twitter account, so follow her **@TheOrdsallGhost – if you dare!**

THE CLEGG HALL BOGGART

One Greater Manchester ghost is so well established and well known that it has been given its own name! Clegg Hall is a dramatic 17th-century hall in Littleborough in Greater Manchester. If you ever visit Clegg Hall, listen out for a strange voice which sounds as if it is giving you a warning. This is a sad tale which has its roots in allegedly true events from many years ago.

The story begins when the master of the house travelled off to join the Crusades. The bad uncle of the family got into the house. He then took the son and daughter of the family and threw them over the battlements into the moat. It was thought that the uncle believed that the master of the house would not return from the Crusades. But he did and the uncle then plotted to murder his brother. As he was about to kill him while he lay sleeping, one of the children's voices was heard to cry out 'Look out father!' and the man woke up and killed his brother. Since then, the children have been heard to issue their warnings to visitors to the hall.

THE MOST HAUNTED THEATRE IN THE COUNTRY?

Oldham Coliseum Theatre is an impressive building which has a varied history going all the way back to 1885. But it seems that the theatre could be haunted by much more than the ghosts of performances past. The well-established theatre has played host to actors as well known as Ralph Fiennes, Dame Thora Hird, Charlie Chaplin and Minnie Driver. But it is also reputed to play host to a ghost or two! In fact, its reputation as the 'most haunted theatre in the country' was so well established that an episode of Most Haunted was filmed there!

OUR TIP? Watch out if you're at the theatre on a Thursday because this is the day that its resident apparition is said to appear most frequently . . . It's all because of the **Scottish Play**, as superstitious actors prefer to refer to **Macbeth**; that is, apart from one actor, Harold Norman. It was while Harold was working at the Coliseum in 1947 that he refused to abide by the unwritten rules of actorly superstition and referred to the play by its actual name as well as rehearsing his lines out loud. Oddly enough, during a fight scene on stage one night, Harold was accidently stabbed with a real sword. Bad luck or something worse? Well, it does make you wonder when you hear that the wound, though treated in hospital, became infected and led to the unfortunate demise of the actor.

Since then, Harold's phantom has been seen at the theatre in the circle area, keeping an eye on the performances of his fellow actors. Employees at the theatre are said to have heard odd noises such as banging doors and even experienced objects mysteriously falling on them. The reason Harold is said to be seen more on Thursdays than any other day of the week? It was reportedly the day that he died . . .

But Harold's ghost isn't the only one thought to haunt the Coliseum Theatre. In the 1970s, a long-standing employee of the theatre, Carl Paulsen, died. Since then, employees have noticed appearances in the wardrobe department by a phantom figure that looks strangely like him. There are even rumours that Buffalo Bill haunts the theatre! No, not that one, but a Wild West actor who worked in the theatre at the start of the 20th century.

Ghost Dog...

LOCAL CUSTOMS

As you would expect in an area so rich in history, Manchester boasts some intriguing customs and traditions. While some, like Molly Dancing, are just a distant memory, others have not only been revived but are now a popular draw for visitors as well as locals! It's no surprise that Ramsbottom's unusual competition involving black pudding and Yorkshire pudding has become famous across the world or that its annual egg-rolling event has enjoyed a strong following for many years. The fact that so many of these customs continue today is perhaps a sign of Manchester's pride in its varied history.

RUSH BEARING

Rush bearing was a tradition that, while not unique to Manchester, still played an important part in its history. It was a church custom in which rushes were placed on the floor of the parish church. People would first gather and process around their parish, carrying rushes. Their journey would conclude at the parish church, where they would then put them on the floor of the church to replace worn-out rushes. Rush bearing went on to become accompanied by festivals and various kinds of entertainment. Once common in many parts of

Rush Bearing MANCHESTER LIBRARIES

Molly dancing MANCHESTER LIBRARIES

England in the 10th century, it was banned in the Victorian age because it was considered to drive people to drunkenness and debauchery! Fortunately, this interesting custom has been brought back to life today in some areas of Greater Manchester, such as Saddleworth.

MOLLY DANCING

May Day was the date for another custom which was popular in Manchester and Greater Manchester many years ago. While girls went out in formal white dresses and carrying broomsticks meant to symbolise maypoles, the boys dressed up in girls' clothing and coloured their faces. They were called Molly Dancers.

PACE EGGING

Eggs are central to an old custom practised in parts of Greater Manchester and elsewhere, even today. Pace Egging made the humble egg the focus of a religious tradition during Easter. The word 'Pace' is thought to come from the Latin word 'Pacha', which means Easter. Pace Egging actually goes back many years and is far from unique to Lancashire. Pace Eggs were traditionally prepared for the Easter festival by being wrapped in onionskins and gently boiled to give them a distinctive golden look. Pace Eggs were enjoyed as part of breakfast on Easter Sunday, kept as decorations or given to groups of performers, known as Pace Eggers (or Jolly Boys), who travelled around villages in the north of England. The Pace Egging Play usually involved St George, a battle and a character called Old Tosspot! While Pace Eggs and Pace Egging were once nearly forgotten, there has been a revival, even if the eggs are now painted rather than wrapped in onion skin! While Pace Egging is no longer part of Easter celebrations for most of us, you can still see the plays performed the traditional way in Middleton and Mossley in Greater Manchester.

Pace Eggers MANCHESTER LIBRARIES

Black Pudding Throwing CREATIVE COMMONS

BLACK PUDDING THROWING

Black pudding throwing is an ancient part of the history of Ramsbottom in Bury. At the annual Black Pudding Throwing Championship, contestants throw three black puddings each at a pile of 21 Yorkshire puddings set on a six-metre plinth. The winner is the person who succeeds in knocking down the highest number of Yorkshire puddings in three goes!

EGG ROLLING

Ramsbottom is the site of yet another intriguing Greater Manchester custom, this time involving eggs. Every Good Friday, people gather at the foot of the town's Holcombe Hill. Both adults and children happily take part in an egg rolling 'eggtravanza' with boiled eggs. The event has become such a big draw that around 3,000 people turn up at the pub at the bottom of the hill! This has understandably led to complaints from local residents and to restrictions being imposed by the local council.

Lancashire Day LANCASHIRE ARCHIVES

LANCASHIRE DAY

The people of Manchester and Greater Manchester take immense pride in celebrating Lancashire Day every 27 November. But what exactly is Lancashire Day? Well, it commemorates the day in 1295 when Lancashire sent its first representatives to a new Parliament initiated by King Edward I of England which went on to become known as The Model Parliament. First observed in 1996 with the loyal toast to 'The Queen, Duke of Lancaster', the people of Manchester join the rest of their region in celebrating with special events and town criers reading out the Lancashire Day proclamation across the county.

LOCAL SPORTS

When you think of Manchester, it's hard not to think of sport, whether it's the reputations of two leading football clubs or the name of a cutting-edge sports facility. Manchester is home to the National Squash Centre, the internationally famous cricket ground Old Trafford and many other sporting venues. With a history featuring swimming baths that are recognised as nationally significant and the start of the world's first professional football league, it is clear that Manchester and sport are a winning combination.

HOME OF WORLD-CLASS FOOTBALL

Say the name Manchester and football inevitably springs to mind. That's thanks to two major teams connected to the city. No prizes for guessing who they are! **Manchester United** and **Manchester City** are closely wrapped up with the history and reputation of Manchester. Despite the rivalries between the two teams, they both continue to represent the city across the world.

The Etihad Stadium - Home of Manchester City SHUTTERSTOCK/DEBU55Y

MANCHESTER CITY

Manchester United is not the only football team to make Mancunians proud. Of course, Manchester City has had its ups and downs in recent times, but in 2011, the club qualified for the UEFA Champions League and won the FA Cup. In 2012, Manchester City won the Premier League, their first league title for 44 years, and they repeated the feat two years later, after local rivals United had regained the trophy in the interim.

Despite their rivalry, Man City and Man U together have helped to raise the profile of Manchester and to make many fans and supporters very happy over the years.

MANCHESTER UNITED

Whatever team you support, you can't deny that Manchester United have had some incredible achievements. No wonder the team is so popular across the world. Did you know that Manchester United began as the Newton Heath Lancashire and Yorkshire Railway Football Club? Fortunately, the club changed its name in 1902. What an amazing history it's had since it began. In all, United have won twenty league titles, two more than Liverpool and seven more than Arsenal, as well as eleven FA Cups and four League Cups! They've also won the European Cup/Champions League and won the UEFA Cup Winners' Cup once and the UEFA Super Cup once!

SHUTTERSTOCK/WARASIT PHOTHISUK

A vintage Manchester United MANCHESTER LIBRARIES

IN THE SWIM

Manchester is also home to what is considered to be the most famous swimming baths in the country, the Victoria Baths. Known as 'Manchester's Water Palace' the baths are now a major source of pride for Mancunians, being recognised as the finest example of swimming pool architecture anywhere in the country. The Grade II listed baths' fascinating history took a downturn when they were closed in 1993. Happily their restoration is now under way, with £3.4 million funding won through the TV series Restoration. The restoration is not yet complete, but Victoria Baths sometimes plays host to festivals and special events. While the baths need even more funding for restoration, their future is looking bright once more.

Victoria Baths MANCHESTER LIBRARIES

GREAT CITY GAMES MANCHESTER

Manchester continues to help lead the way in sport, thanks to its involvement in the Great City Games. Held in Manchester and other cities, they bring leading sports events right to the city centre. Great City Games events are hosted in temporary, purpose-built outside arenas, featuring a specially constructed IAAF certified four-lane sprint track, allowing people to get closer to sports. Locals can watch world-class athletes competing in sports such as long jump, pole vaulting, sprinting and hurdling in the heart of Manchester.

BOXING HERITAGE

Manchester boxers have achieved a great deal over the last one hundred years, from superstars like Jackie Brown to legends like Ricky Hatton.

FEEL THE CHILL

Did you know that Manchester is the home to what is the UK's longest and the world's widest real snow indoor ski slope? At Chill Factore, Mancunians can enjoy everything from skiing to snowboarding to climbing at the indoor Alpine Village.

MANCHESTER LIBRARIES

LOCAL HISTORY

> *"Manchester is the place where people do things. Don't talk about what you are going to do, do it. That is the Manchester habit. And through the manifestation of this quality, the word Manchester has become a synonym for energy and freedom and the right to think and to do without shackles."*

JUDGE PARRY

Manchester has played an important part in the history of Britain and the world. It's a place whose influences span from household names in music to a leading role in the Industrial Revolution. Manchester has had an impact on many different aspects of everyday life since its early existence as a township.

HUMBLE BEGINNINGS

Manchester is a familiar name throughout the world, but from where does the city actually derive its name? According to Oxford University Press, the city takes its name from *Mamucium*, which was the Roman name for a first-century settlement and fort built there in AD79. However, Manchester is often given the Latin name of Mancuniun.

A RADICAL HISTORY

'What Manchester does today, the rest of the world does tomorrow.'

BENJAMIN DISRAELI

Manchester is the birthplace of many radical movements which have helped make life better for people today. It's a place whose history is marked by a struggle for progress. One key event was the terrible massacre of Peterloo which took place on 16 August 1819. On that day, 60,000 peaceful protesters had gathered on St Peter's Fields in Manchester to demand the right to elect their own MPs and to hear talks by radical speakers. When the Manchester Yeomanry arrived to arrest the speakers, clashes started between the Yeomanry and the crowds. The Hussars were then sent in. Eleven people died and over 600 people were wounded. The massacre was named Peterloo in an ironic echo of the Battle of Waterloo. Historians acknowledge that Peterloo was hugely influential in giving ordinary men the vote and enabling the rise of the Chartist movement which supported the creation of the trade unions.

Manchester also had an important part to play in the struggle for women's rights. In 1858, the city was the birthplace of Emmeline Goulden who, as Emmeline Pankhurst, established the Women's Franchise League, which fought to allow married women to vote in local elections. Emmeline went on to set up the more militant Women's Social and Political Union (WSPU), whose members were the first to be called 'Suffragettes'. Finally, in 1918, the Representation of the People Act gave voting rights to women over 30. It was an important start.

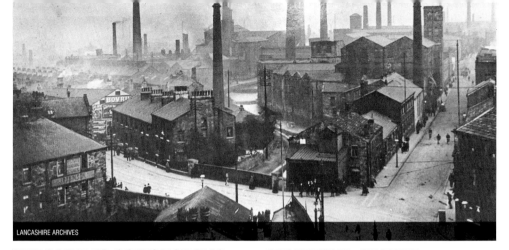

LANCASHIRE ARCHIVES

WELCOME TO COTTONOPOLIS

How could the Industrial Revolution have happened without Manchester? The city lay right at the heart of this crucial series of events which changed industry for ever. By the 18th century, Manchester was the cotton-making capital of the world. The city of Manchester was so much part of the cotton industry that it was known to the locals as 'Cottonopolis'. Cottonopolis created jobs for many people and was home to industrial innovations which went on to change the way we lived.

INDUSTRIAL CHANGE

It was in Manchester in 1781 that Richard Arkwright opened the first steam-driven textile mill the world had ever seen. It was also Manchester, combined with towns in south and east Lancashire, which quickly became the world's largest and most productive cotton spinning centre. The city was also the location of the very first industrial suburb centred on steam power, Ancoats.

A FAST TRACK TO THE FUTURE

Manchester wasn't just a leading player in the history of industry in the 17th, 18th and 19th centuries. The city also became a key transport hub with the creation of the Bridgewater Canal, which enabled the transport of bulk quantities of goods to the Castlefield terminus. The canal became the central route for huge quantities of raw cotton moved through the port of Liverpool from many different locations across the world. Manchester's railway network also grew to meet the demands of industry. In 1894 the Manchester Ship Canal opened, turning Manchester into an inland port.

BUZZING

The worker bee is the highly appropriate symbol for Manchester, chosen during the Industrial Revolution. It's a symbol of hard work and industry. You'll notice the bee on

MANCHESTER LIBRARIES

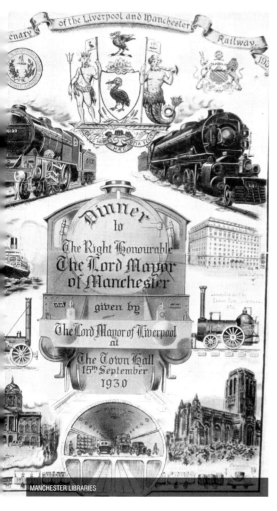

MANCHESTER LIBRARIES

the city's coat of arms, which were granted to the Borough of Manchester in 1842. The symbol gives HMS Manchester its nickname of 'Busy Bee'. You can also spot the bee on the crest of the ship. No prizes for finding the bee on the Boddingtons Brewery logo and on the coat of arms of the University of Manchester.

CONCILIO ET LABORE

MUSIC CITY

No history of Manchester would be complete without a look at its significant contribution to music. Think Manchester and you may think of Oasis, Take That, Happy Mondays, The Charlatans or many other important acts. While Manchester's 'Madchester' days of the 1980s and 1990s certainly helped to bring a lot of joy to many people, Manchester has always been a leader when it comes to great music.

SOME OF MANCHESTER'S MUSIC
GREATS INCLUDE:

HAPPY MONDAYS

HERMAN'S HERMITS

THE BEE GEES

BLACK GRAPE

ELKIE BROOKS

THE CHEMICAL BROTHERS

DOVES

ELBOW

THE FALL

THE HOLLIES

JOY DIVISION

M PEOPLE

THE SMITHS

JOHNNY MARR

NEW ORDER

CORONATION STREET

For many people, no look at the history of Manchester would be complete without a mention of Coronation Street. Whether or not you're a fan of the long-running TV soap, it's fair to say that 'The Street' has brought many distinctive characters to our TV screens since it first aired on Granada Television in December 1960. The programme portrays 'everyday' life in a fictional Manchester town, Weatherfield, based on Salford. Not that these characters' lives are particularly everyday! Well, it is a soap opera . . . No one could have anticipated the long-lived success of the programme which started out as a pilot of just 13 episodes, or that within only six months it had turned into the most-watched TV programme on British television! Featuring beloved characters such as Deirdre Barlow, Bet Lynch and Fred Elliott, 'Corrie' continues to hook in audiences every

The cast of Coronation Street SHUTTERSTOCK/FEATUREFLASH

week. The Coronation Street set was alongside the former Granada TV headquarters, close to Manchester city centre, but recently a new set has been built at Trafford Wharf. For a limited time it's possible to book a tour of the original set, but failing that, if you head to the second floor of the Museum of Science and Industry, you can still just about catch a glimpse of the world famous street . . .

MANCHESTER'S HISTORY:
TEN FASCINATING FACTS

1. Manchester was the world's first industrial city.

2. Manchester became the birthplace of one of the most iconic car brands in the world in 1904 when Frederick Royce and Charles Rolls arranged a meeting at the Midland Hotel and went on to establish Rolls-Royce.

3. The Trade Union Congress was created in The Three Crowns pub in Salford. Its first general meeting took place in 1868 at the Mechanics Institute in Princess Street.

4. It is said that The Midland Hotel was where Hitler wanted his UK headquarters to be!

5. Liverpool Road train station is the oldest surviving terminal railway station. It opened in 1830 and was one of the first two railway passenger terminals in the world. It is now part of the Museum of Science and Industry.

6. The world's first professional football league was set up at the Royal Hotel, Piccadilly in 1888.

7. The Hallé Orchestra, the UK's oldest symphony orchestra (and the fourth oldest in the world), was established in 1857 by German conductor and pianist Charles Hallé.

8. Manchester is home to Chetham's Library, the oldest public library in the English-speaking world, which opened in 1653.

9. The atom was split for the first time by Ernest Rutherford in an experiment at Manchester University in 1919.

10. Opened in 1761, Manchester's Bridgewater Canal was the first artificial waterway which was fully independent of natural rivers.

A HISTORY IN BUILDINGS

Manchester is packed with some historic architectural gems which reveal something of its vibrant past. Just three of them are:

Chetham's Library

The oldest surviving public library in Britain was created by banker and textile merchant, Sir Humphrey Chetham. Constructed in 1421, it was originally built to provide a base for a college of priests, and is the oldest complete structure in Manchester.

Chetham's goal? To establish the first place of independent study in the north of England. He stipulated in his will that the building should become a charity school and a free public library. With over 70,000 books, Chetham's now specialises in the history and topography of Greater Manchester and Lancashire.

MANCHESTER LIBRARIES

Manchester Town Hall

This neo-gothic building was completed in 1877 after the old town hall became too small for local government to use. It was built as the result of a competition which was won by architect Alfred Waterhouse.

The building required no fewer than 14 million bricks and cost about the equivalent of £70 million today! The town hall was officially opened in 1877 though Queen Victoria chose not to attend.

Manchester Town Hall ANDY SUSAN CAFFREY

The Free Trade Hall

Now a hotel, the Free Trade Hall in Peter Street was created to commemorate the repeal of the Corn Laws in 1846. The Grade II listed building is built on St Peter's Fields, the site of the Peterloo massacre. The hall was funded by public subscription. Another interesting part of its history is that it went on to be used as a concert hall and as the base for the Hallé Orchestra in 1858. The hall has also been the site for historic addresses and performances by figures as varied as Bob Dylan, Charles Dickens and Winston Churchill.

The Free Trade Hall SHUTTERSTOCK/ALASTAIR WALLACE

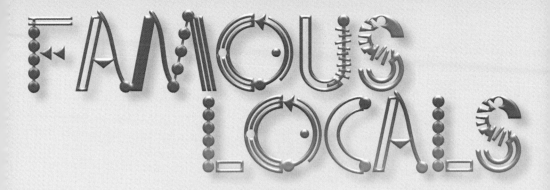

FAMOUS LOCALS

SHUTTERSTOCK/MELIS

SIR ALEX FERGUSON

Despite not being originally from Manchester, Sir Alex Ferguson was recently named as Manchester's greatest ever sporting legend! This is thanks to his brilliant career managing Manchester United from 1986 to 2013.

Sir Alex is the longest-serving manager of Manchester United. He has won countless awards and holds a whole array of records, such as winning Manager of the Year the highest number of times in British football history.

EMMELINE PANKHURST

Manchester's Moss Side was the birthplace of a central figure in the Suffragette movement. Emmeline Pankhurst helped to change women's history for ever by setting up the Women's Social and Political Union which went on to become the feminist movement known as 'the Suffragettes'.

MANCHESTER LIBRARIES

MORRISSEY

Steven Patrick Morrissey, better known as Morrissey, is one of Manchester's most famous sons. This talented and often controversial figure grew in fame in the 1980s as the lyricist and vocalist of The Smiths and then went on to have a successful solo career. Born in Davyhulme, Greater Manchester in 1959 to a hospital porter father and librarian mother, Morrissey continues to be one of the best-known and bequiffed products of Manchester.

MICHELLE KEEGAN

Michelle Keegan, born in Stockport in 1987, is best known as Tina McIntyre in Coronation Street. While Michelle recently left the series, it's clear that she won't be away from our TV screens for very long!

SHUTTERSTOCK FEATUREFLASH

MANCHESTER LIBRARIES

SIR JOSEPH WHITWORTH

You can't go to many places in Manchester without encountering the name Whitworth. No wonder, when you consider the impact of Stockport-born Sir Joseph Whitworth.

Not content with being an engineer and businessman, Whitworth was also an active philanthropist. His generosity to the people of Manchester after his death is part of the reason that locals and visitors alike benefit from the Whitworth Art Gallery and Christie Hospital.

PAUL SCHOLES

Think Manchester United and you can't helping thinking of Paul Scholes, a Mancunian who played his entire professional footballing career for United. Now retired, Scholes will continue to be a significant name in sport for many years to come. This is because of his brilliant career in football, which saw him play a key part in the club's treble-winning success in the 1998–99 season. Scholes is also famous for winning no fewer than 11 Premier League, three FA Cup and two UEFA Champions League winners' medals. In total, Scholes made over 700 appearances for United, which is the third-highest number of appearances by any player for the club, even returning from retirement to assist in the successful Premier League campaign in 2012–13.

SIR JOSEPH JOHN 'J. J.' THOMSON

Manchester boasts 25 Nobel Prize winners. One of them is Sir Joseph

John 'J. J.' Thomson, who was born in Cheetham Hill in 1856. During his illustrious career, Thomson was able to demonstrate that cathode rays were made of what was previously an unknown negatively charged particle and also found the very first evidence for isotopes of a stable element. In 1906 Thomson was awarded the Nobel Prize in Physics for his discovery of the electron and for his achievements in investigating the conduction of electricity in gases.

NOEL GALLAGHER

Along with his brother Liam, Noel Gallagher is one of Manchester's best-known musical celebrities. It all began in the 1960s in Burnage. After starting to learn guitar at the age of thirteen, Noel went on to become involved in the city's music scene. Later on, as the lead guitarist and songwriter, he joined the band that Liam had formed, which became Oasis. Oasis was a big part of the soundtrack of the 1990s, along with another Britpop band, Blur, with which Oasis publicly feuded. The Gallagher brothers have famously fought over the years. It was one of these fights that led to the end of Oasis. Noel has since pursued a solo career, forming his own band, Noel Gallagher's High Flying Birds, in 2011.

SHUTTERSTOCK/FEATUREFLASH

Lowry Gallery SHUTTERSTOCK/ALI KHAN

L.S. LOWRY

Think Manchester and art and you'll probably find that distinctive stick figures come to mind. That's because Rusholme-born L.S. Lowry is so much part of the history of Manchester, particularly Salford. Famous for his atmospheric paintings of industrial scenes in Northern England (and those stick figures), Lowry's art and reputation is still going strong today. But this isn't something for which Lowry would have cared. Lowry rejected five honours throughout his life, including a knighthood in 1968, which makes it interesting to wonder what he would have made of the purpose-built Lowry Gallery and adjoining Lowry Outlet Mall on Salford Quays.

ALBERT FINNEY

Born in Salford in 1936, Albert Finney has gone on to become one of the acting world's most familiar faces, with roles in films as varied as Saturday Night and Sunday Morning, Big Fish, The Bourne Ultimatum, The Bourne Legacy and Skyfall. Finney is a dedicated supporter of Manchester United. He was the narrator for the documentary Munich, which told the tragic story of the air crash that killed most of the Busby Babes in 1958.

SIR EDWIN ALLIOTT VERDON ROE

Sir Alliott Verdon Roe took Manchester's reputation sky high, quite literally. This pioneering individual was born in Patricroft, Eccles in 1877. Not content with being a leading aircraft manufacturer, he went on to become the very first Englishman to fly an all-British plane.

MANCHESTER LIBRARIES

RICHARD COBDEN

Richard Cobden was another historic figure who, though not born in Manchester, was to have a significant influence within it and further afield. Born in Heyshott, Cobden became MP for Stockport in 1841. He was recognised as being one of the central figures in the founders of the Anti-Corn Law League. This was important because the harsh Corn Laws increased the cost of bread, affecting the lives of society's most vulnerable people. When the Corn Laws were abolished in 1846, Cobden was celebrated as a local hero, with a statue going up in his honour in Manchester's St Ann's Square in 1865.

MANCHESTER LIBRARIES